THE

Susan Joy Menchell

DEDICATION

To all the women who have inspired me to be
open with my feelings and my writing:

Doris Menchell

Faith Pollack

Karen Sillas

Joanne Angel Barry Colon

Aphrodite Mirisis

Contents

Time for Making Love

Heart all akimbo
How do you know
What it is I'm feeling
Rocking and rolling
To keep up the show
The usual front
Do you ever find
What it is
You're lookin' for—
Or are these just
Lyrics to a song?

Heart all akimbo
Hey I think I know
What it is
I'm looking for –
He won't be perfect
Yet he'll be steadfast
And kind at the same time
And there'll be no
    game playing.
There'll be only
Time
For making love.

Paradise

Between your thighs
You say "is paradise"
I know the lies
I know the lines
And see the disguise
You think you hide.

You carry dreams
From girl to girl
Giving them a whirl
Hoping one will stay
Without a thought
Of their hearts.

You kindle fires
With the look in your eyes
You leave quickly
Without a disguise
Into the night
Like a hurt alley cat.

What kind of paradise
   is that;
No promises, no line
I'll be feeling fine
With you, without you
Because peace is mine
Peace is becoming mine.

To Truly Love

My tears are of blood and sweat.
Red and salty
Unable am I to see
Any more pain through them.

My heart aches wanting
   so badly
To stop and rest
To remember joy and laughter
Rather than guilt and shame.

And you run away always
Yet, claiming you feel only pure love
That to me is as salt on an open wound—
Certainly far from painless

And I bleed each day
As you watch, unmoved
Unknowing of what it is
It takes to truly love.

Towers ("Ground Zero")

Crumbling falling down
Once magnificent
Steel strongest metal
Falling crumbling into dust
Lives destroyed
Human beings
Flying from great heights
Flames and heat
Charred bodies
As if a battlefield
Suddenly appeared
From what was a money pit, a metropolis
Where people sold and bought
Bargaining for their lives
Little did they know
Planes sent onto paths
To destroy all.

Last rites
Last phone calls
To say "I love you"
Our New York
Our people, our love
Turned into grief
In a split second
Floor by Floor tumbling
Plane parts and bodies
Igniting and then gone

Death death by the thousands
Something no one could anticipate
Nothing to be done
Except to save the living
Bleeding, broken
Shocked lost
Ambling across bridges
By foot—over miles
To get to safety
Hospitals waiting
Mostly in vain
For the living

No one untouched
Fear, anger, frustration
Loss that was unexpected
Inexplicable pain
Families left devastated
Businesses destroyed
Firemen, police, doctors
Left working in 24-hour shifts
To save the living.
Ground zero.

The Sparrow

The sparrow sings to you
But although you hear her
You don't cherish her differences
With a soul that makes her
Separate from all the others
She sings a song uniquely for you,
But you don't hear the difference
Between hers and all the other voices.

Her voice is filled with a spirit
That cannot be captured
Cannot be tamed
And although you do not understand
You will be enlightened
By feeling your own freedom
By knowing you are loved
By knowing the truth
Is in the simplest pleasures
The sun
The earth
And the moon.

The sparrow sings to you
As you find your way
And until you learn to listen
With a whole heart
You will never know the beauty
Of her voice.

Home

I wanna go home
To age five
With grandma by my side
House always smelling
Of lilacs in summertime
And of roast chicken
Or turkey or ham,
I can feel her
Holding my hand
On Queens Boulevard
We are two women
Going to lunch
I'm five.

Going on thirty-five
Walking in the diner
With Grandma Rose
(my best friend)
A person I would
Continue to love
And always remember
Long after she'd passed.

I see her
In front of me
She is strong
We sit
Playing canasta
While we sip our tea
Wearing her favorite green dress
Made just for her
(She'd sewn it herself).
Her pearl earrings
Strong yet gentle
Always there for me
I thought she'd live forever.

Yes, I wanna be five
And watch Grandma
Cut roses in the backyard again
And see her smile
And love her some more.

Stop Shorts

The naked tree branch
Reaches out to me in mid
Winter

The water on the tree branch
Freezes
Turning into icicles

Birds sing in the morning sun;
In autumn.

The moon, the star, and I
Underneath.

A shadow on my blinds
A lone pine tree

Winter winds
    push
Autumn leaves aside

The cat warms itself under
The car engine

Sun rising pokes itself through
My closed blinds

Spaghetti boils
In a pot of water

Steam from a teapot
warms
my heart

Tick tock clock
beating
in the night

Flowers
   bloom
In autumn

The towers fall
As I watch
The screen,
And cry

Sunday

Boring day so far
Just had to
Walk the dog
Ate something easy
While I wait
For Faith & Mom
To take a walk
My walk
By the Cross Island
From Crocheron Park
Up to the Boulevard
Exactly 2 miles
No less
No more

I wait
For them to arrive
To take a walk
By the water
To see Douglaston Manor

And the boats
In the distance
To wish I was rich
And live there
In a big old house
With the spray
Of the bay
In the yard
The dog bouncing
In our grass
He seems to be
With me dreaming
Bouncing around
The apartment
Eating little bones.

You

Mike you come over
With your royal entrance
Making it seem plain
That you come here
　　Every day.
I don't know what to do
It's not really about you
But the boys
7 & 18. I want to see them
I want them in my life
So I see you too
On Labor Day
And it's my labor of love
I knew there'd be
Some repercussions
But hell.
The divorce isn't final
I shouldn't speak to you.
Oh, hell, it all sucks.

But I got to see
The boys together
So you came
To the barbecue
No harm done.

I have nothing against you.
I am not in this war
I don't like the games.
I'm even glad you came
So they'll sue me
Yell and cry
And try to unglue me
But I'll have better motives
Than they can ever see
Mike
You are not my problem.
Hope you had
A good Labor Day.

The Sun Rises

The sun rises and there's
   an orange glow
Beneath my new sky
A bird flies across the
   Monday canvas
I sit pen in hand after
   so many years
Un-penned remembering
   and forgetting together
How I had forgotten to write
   my thoughts
And once again I begin
   anew with you.

Morning stirs very slowly
   for me today
As if I have forgotten the
   difference
Between night and day
   and gunas and world.

The Dog

The dog runs into the dining
    room
Huge bone in his teeth.
The dog knows to stay in the
    kitchen
Yet wants to show me
        his prize.

The dog is a family member
He has become a big part of
        things.
He must be walked, fed,
        cleaned
And mostly he must be petted.

The dog knows he's loved
The dog questions nothing.
He knows he will be cared for.
What a life this dog has.

Gone

He's dead; gone
The father I once fought
The father I once hated.

He's buried; gone
Done; no more
And yet so much has changed.

Where there he was
   in his chair
No one's seated

Where he once ate
Grandchildren now sit.

He's dead; gone
Amazing to believe
Who once loomed large
Scared me to death.

My father; my enemy
Now lies in a grave
Far from us to see.

He's dead, gone
Who once caused
So much pain
So much hurt

And now to go on
  is confusing
And now to go on
  is work—

No one to criticize
   me
No one to curse, scream
At all life's disappointments
He's gone now—

Simply Living

I see you – I love you
You're always walking away
I see you – as a shadow
I see green eyes, brown hair
But who is it I see inside
Prone to rage when angry
Prone to do good for others
Always arranging some meeting
For others to mingle
Sloppy – never caring about
All those bills we get
All the receipts you get
Going on walking through it
As if life is so simple
As if time is infinite.

I see you – leaving tonight
To go see some live music
To go off into your love
Love of simply living.

You Big Puffed Bird

You big puffed bird
You eat and eat
Never feeling full.
You take and take.
All becomes your prey
Including me
My weaknesses –
You feel all powerful
I've allowed that
And now
What is my fate?
Will you spit me out
   in pieces?
I fear your absence
Yet dread your presence.
I scatter my dreams
Like so much bait –

You big puffed bird
You frighten me
And in the end
Will you win out
Devouring all you see
Feeding on everyone
On all our weaknesses
As if kindness
Were a sort of disease –

We enable you to fly
While we all stay grounded
We enable you not to care
While we care for you.
I see no end
To this cycle
You eat
While we starve.
You fly
While we watch.
What happens
When you've eaten
All we've had
To give you – what then?

Tree of Life

Leaves, once green & supple
Turn to brown and fall
From the tree as I watch
And you once young
Turn old and ill
Lying in the hospital bed
Your body shutting down
Where once a vital being
    stood.

Now you tremble in pain
What's happening we all know
But no one wants to say
There were so many so many
Happier lively days
And we call out to you
But you are fading
You are shedding your skin
As soon you too
Will go from suppleness
To the fall from
The tree of life.

Garina

She had skin of mocha
        color
And eyes deep muddy
        brown
To dive into
Smoking Newport 100's
But so calm and alluring
In her Kinko's uniform.

It's not how she approaches;
It's in how she speaks
So soft and sweet
As a bird
As the wind
And the work is easy.
She is light as a feather
Taking paper and turning it
Turning it into treasure
Turning it into love.

Whipping Girl

I am not your whipping
    girl
Attuned to every nuance of fear
You insist on evoking in
    others.
I am not your borrowed
    slave
Bowing to each request
As I break my spine
To acquiesce to your wishes.

I am no longer there
No longer wanting a
    glance
From a beast like
    you.
I will walk on upright
As you crawl homeward
Back to your stinking mud
    cave
Into the prison of your trap.
You, my dear,
Have lost all humanity
You are slime—

Mules

Mules are the style in
    Pennsylvania State
Horses they say are
  too wild
So you ride a mule thinking
  it's great.

They're awkward; they're
    really second rate
But they're much less tricky
  for a child.
Mules are the style in
  Pennsylvania State.

I've picked Sweet Pea, a real
    "fashion plate".
With her I don't get a
  least bit riled
So you ride a mule thinking
  it's great.

You can even show up late
One leader said as he "bucktoothed"
    smiled
Mules are the style in
  Pennsylvania State.

The tree we walked into
    was just fate
The ground I tumbled to
    no more thrilling than "having piles"
So you ride a mule thinking it's great.

I still took my leader's picture,
Although she couldn't relate
One of her and one of her mule
    for my files
Mules are the style in Pennsylvania State
So you ride a mule thinking it's great.

Dad

You once dominated me—
My heart and soul
Were blackened and cursed
With your madness, your sorrow.

I lived and breathed
Your fears and sorrows.
I cried the tears
You refused to allow.

I channeled you long enough
And letting you go
Was a curse
Now has become
My dream.

I awaken in a new world
With time having passed
And new people by my side.
More possibilities are here
Than I had ever imagined.

Night Air

I arise from near death
Or so it has felt.
I am certain I've seen hell
Though it might be life
At its most tilted pitch.

Suddenly and without warning
There are sparks of joy.
The old lament is gone.
There's that chance
At something so much more.

I sit on my front stoop
And the night air is
    invigorating.
The patio lights spectacular
And dreams of success
    are mine.

Boxed In

You are in a box hidden away
Far away a child cries.
Although you appear content
You are in an old dream,
One that isn't really you.
Suddenly you burst open
Your heart on fire-furious
Glowing red, envious, and shocked.
Truth will do that to you
Truth you feel has lead you away,
But in reality you are awakening
From a long tired dream.

Who are you—
An empty box
Faining joy?
What are you?
A figment
A dream
A nightmare.

You are not
Forthright.
You are not
Above
Judgment.

You have brought
    sorrow
Where you fake
    Happiness
You have released
    chaos
Where you fake
    order.

You are a hypocrite.

A Trail

The army of women
That took apart the rules
And followed a trail
Through once darkened woods
Sits on either side of me.
Unbeknownst to them
I am a sister
And I feel the power
Of all who lead me
Forward to seek my own path
Once dejected and downtrodden.

I seek my own soul.
I seek my own purpose.
I do not live for others
And the drum that beats
Is from inside me,
A beat so strong
No other can take me
Away from my chosen path.

I can see the streams
and open fields I once loved
And flow with them again.
I can hear the wind
Speaking through the distance,
And no longer will I remain
In the shadow of others—

Crossroad

The island I took myself to
Is no longer the safe haven
Of my dreams; I only thought so.
The isolation I sought
Was my punishment
For simply not knowing
What some knew.

I meet you halfway
And you scorn me each time.
I am the person you once saw
Simply terrified of fully being
In that it is too new;
And you and I will not be able
To meet halfway at some point.

If the tables were turned
Would I understand you,
Or is it impossible
For anyone to see me
The way I really am, yet
I stand at the crossroads—

I come from sea to land
And hear all you have to say
But no longer can respond.
I myself have travelled great distances
And searched unendingly for peace of mind;
Yet no one understands yet.
It is not them I look for or need
It is simply myself I have misused.

Tunnel

Tunnelling into the heart
Right to the center
Of where all our fears
Begin and end.
You have no trouble
Seeing into mine
But me; I am lost
And I am saddened.
It is difficult
And dreams are lost
Over and over again
Each time
I think of my
Weaknesses—

Never Meant For You

I cleanse you from inside of
   me
And yet your soul refuses to
   leave.
You feign being gone to scorn me
Yet I know you
And I know you'll be back
To fool and baffle me again.

I see you
Looking through the stars
At me
And I know
The trees
Scream with your energy.

You know I suffer
And yet
You cannot fathom
The depths
Of my loss.

I am your heart
And you have stolen
A piece of my soul
Never meant for you.

You Used To Be

You used to be,
A friend of mine
And what happened
I do not understand.
You are strange
And unwise
Uncertain and unclear
On whom you are seeing.

You once knew me
To be kind and thoughtful
And now I find you
Odd and self-seeking.
Who is it I once knew
You or someone else
I wish I understood
What you want—

Blue

In the blue of the moon
I saw your eyes
And the pain of hiding
I once knew too
Beckoned me
To love you.
You thwarted me though,
And I find
Some changes—
My mind has made
Because of the uncertainty
Of you

The time that's gone by
And your
Broken dreams
And broken heart
Beckon me
To find you
Somehow, some way.
And finally
I think I am too late.
I think you're gone.
You aren't the man
I thought you were.
You are only someone
I imagined.

Bells

There are no ties, no times, no flights
    of fancy
There are no old connections, just voices
    of new, new voices
New dreams, new places and a leaving
A leaving behind of all you once felt—
    "I felt"
I can see the light blazing a path
Behind trees where my soul once sunk.
I keep the distances of travel
All tolled into my soul
So that I may dream
And climb out of the abyss
And not into the stiffness
Of too much structure.

I stay free, always free
Loving the breeze on my cheek.
The taste of good food and dreams
And the colors that blend
Into visions when you close
Your eyes and envision
The light of the sun internally,
And we know the endlessness
Of freedom
Of bells ringing
That haven't ever been rung before.

Tingle

Tingle of water
In a tub
Full of bubbles.
Baby puts them
On her head
And becomes
A unicorn,
And mama
Laughs

Baby
Touches
Stars that are reflections
Of light
In the water
And smiles—

There are seashells
In her future
And sand will be
Between her toes,
But for now
She is a child
With bubbles
In a tub
And mom
By her side—

Seekers

Almost gone from all that
    existed
I take flight in your
    leaving—
I take flight on your
    suggestions.
I am no longer the
    slave.
To a feeling that no longer
    makes sense.

Your demons were also mine.
Your pain became mine,
And I have opened the box
And set free souls that entrapped
    themselves.
For no reason
Other than they felt
Unallowed to present themselves
    fully
Into the place
They belonged
Into the world
Among others
Who would have
All the heart
To embrace them.

Souls among other wondering souls—
Dreamers among other dreamers
Life seekers looking through
   each other's perceptions
Life seekers learning to let
  the dead
Lie dead and buried
And to seek all the energy
And all the light
We are able to amass
In the world
That we have not dreamed up
But the world we have
   discovered
Simply by living in it.

All You Had

The chocolate milk
And the kind words
Only held up for so long
And you tried—
How hard you tried
To keep a hold on me,
But I left you too soon
Always you felt; too soon
And now I know it too.
The pain in your trembling heart
At the child you were unable to see
And the one who refused to be held.

I remember how I ran
Out the doors of your house.
It never was my house.
I refused to be a part
I refused to be yours;
Though I know you wanted it.
I never was really like you
Never stood for anything other
  than myself.
I can't bleed for you now
  though
And it must be put into words,
For the chocolate milk and kind
  words
I know now—is all you had.

The Secret

Close your eyes
And know
I'm always inside
And always beside
    you;
Filling you with
The love
I always had.

I will never
Forget
The way
That you loved me
And the secret
We shared
That only
A brother and sister
Could know—

A New Vision

Feathers fall
Like rain
And time
Becomes trite
And overplayed
Like the words
to your favorite songs
That once were
So important
Yet no longer
Are meaningful;
And suddenly
A flame
From a candle
Brings you
  Back
To a room
  Back
With another
You once
Loved
  Back then.

And you see
That candle
Over and over
   Back through time
As if birth years
And birthdays
Passed
And keep
Passing
Backwards
In your
  mind
Where
Once were
Great ideas
And images
That could
Travel
You
Through
Space and
  time.

Now
You stop
Stop suddenly
    are
At an impass
A crossroad
Awaiting
Sitting and waiting
For a new
  vision.

Welcome to My Resistance

You are the lock
And I am the key
You are the barrier
To me finding me.
You are the fear
I chose never to bear,
You are the grief
That I feel
Whenever I am there.

You are the error.
You are the anger.
You are the thing
I refuse to change
Though it drives me
   insane—
You, you are me
And my resistance to change.

I've Tried

--To J.N.

I've tried to please
        you
    worship you
    and need you
And I've died little
    deaths
    1000 times.
I'm feeling broken and
    abused, used
    and forsaken.
Didn't you know what
    it was—
        that confused you?
I tried too hard too much
    too often
To take away "your" pain
A pain you'll need
    to take with you
In order to grow,
But I'm only sorry
I didn't know sooner.

For Kevin

I walked through snowy
   streets
  of Boston with you
As if my suitcase
   was in my
     hand.
In each and every step I took
You, you had come to
    live and
    enjoy
And I to let some
  part of me
  die.
It's hard I know
   to watch
   another's pain
As you did in the
   hospital corridor
Having such a stiff
   upper lip
And still loving me
Just the way you
Looked in my eyes;
And for that I
  will
Keep you in my
  heart
Although I let you
  walk away
Again
Not so long ago.

I Dreamt

I dreamt I was a bird
You know how I always
   loved trees
Well I was winged and
   free.
My spirit soared and
   I landed.
I was with humans but
   not among them.

I fly without a purpose
Yet I now know
What it is to be free.
I fly without a home
But I have left
The cage I once was
   locked into.

I am free
Without trouble
Without blame.
I need no names
No label
No disguise.

When again I look
Into your eyes
You will know
No veils exist
Inside anymore.

I remember all
Yet am so far away
From the shell
I once hid in.
I was that shell;
You were right.

Now I soar
Over weaknesses
That were my weight.
I am slowly
Changing
And building my self.

As feathers fall
The night air
Beneath my wings
Lifts me out of
    sight
And I am rising
Over oceans and mountains
Just as I had
    dreamt
Long ago.

The Two Selves

What am I—spirit or
    flesh--?
How do they meet
    within me--?
I feel a soul at
    war,
Spirit searching for
    freedom,
Flesh searching for
    love.

I am not sure
How the two
Will settle.

Body

This body is some burden
I carry it and carry it
But never marry it
To my soul
  (somewhere else, I suppose).

I fret at each lump
And each imperfection;
Yet I know it gets worse,
So why don't I let go?

You know I once was a teen
With skinny hips in tight jeans.
I once strutted like a cat
Followed by a trail of suitors' eyes.

Why, oh why
Do you own a thing
That you never chose?
How'd this come to be me?

And I dress,
Fluff my hair
Make-up here,
Push up there

Where has my importance
Begun and ended
Inside or out?

Is this a trap
Or a vehicle?
I might change my
    stride—
Should something
    inside
Be allowed to come
    out.
I used to shout
And now I whisper
Even to myself.

This body is my
    way
To say
Or do
All that I need to.

And I guess
This body
Is a place
I guess
To hide
Or even
To rest.

Will You Remember Me?

I remember you
Every day now
(I'll have to come visit).
I remember us
Every hour now.
I'll no longer need to cry
(I sometimes laugh
At how we danced,
At how you always
Held my hand).

You were my first love
   Ira
Unafraid of course
Because you loved me so
Me—unafraid because you'd
   do anything
To make me happy, to make
   me laugh.

I lost you
Very quickly
As if you had never existed.
I lost myself
In a sea of confusion
And hatred (towards our
    father).

I forgot for too long
How that love,
My first love, felt.
I remember you
Every day now.
Will you remember me?

Earned My Own Wings

Life baby, has ripped
    my heart open
So I no longer need
    the figures
Or any facts - to
        know
What it is I feel.
I can't reach you.
I know this now
And accept this,
And I bleed
One last tear,
For now I must heal
And I will heal alone.
I can see how hard
It is to finally be free
For I have
Finally earned
My own wings—

I

Who I was with you
We both know
Was not who I am.

I tried to tell you
"All we have is now",
Yet you'd never understand.

A hand is a touch.
A kiss is a heart.
None can hold time.

The sky fills with stars.
The sun then returns
While we sleep,
We take it for granted.

The changes are cycles
And continue on

We mark time on calendars
And pray for internal peace
Bombarded with external chaos.

We are soldiers
In the war
Of our own creation.

When we have forsaken
Our childhood illusion,
We learn to use emotion
In our own favor,
Displaying as we choose
And keeping much to our
    selves.

Who I was
Will never be again,
And thank God
For who I am becoming
For she is the child,
    the prodigy,
Of my own soul's
    making.
She is the result
    of much work.

And who I am
No longer requires
The "OK's" from others.
The attention a child
    seeks;

Instead I stand alone.

For Ira

I see you in all corners of
   the world
And your love inspires
   me
To begin over again
Without a care
Without any desperation.
I need only the
   calm
Of a sea breeze
And a new sun.

I see you with a
   new vision
For a future without
   regret,
A future where all dreams
   are possible.

My Three Friends

Something changed
    tonight.
What I thought were
    sad remains
Of whom I had been
Came to life,
Circling around
My stubborn heart
And rose to a high
    pitch
Of unremembered pleasures.

Smiles and laughing.
Jim, John and Carl
Making punch,
Lining up all the bottles
Of booze,
And posing behind them,
While I took the picture.
My men
My three loves and mostly
My three friends.

Jimmy V. calling me
At home
Begging to know
If what I had on
Was see-through.
Of course, I said "yes".

John, trying to stay
    overnight,
The door I had to
    slam
Behind him,
Yet remained open,
As friends.

And Carl
Football jersey lent
Almost kissed me
But I couldn't ever
Betray

My only bass-player
    lover and friend;
And supreme
Spontaneous animal:
Jimmy V.

I have the photo to
Remember you all by.

And I hope you'll all
Always remember
    as well.

The Stage

My life has become an
   empty stage now
Without you and I to
   carry on,
And no matter how
   angry you've made me
      in the past
I miss the twinkle in
   your green eyes
As you teach me to hike up
   the 90° mountain,
As you turn from your horse
   to smile and look at me
      riding behind you.

It's those things I want to
   remember
But they tear my heart
   in two
Right now,
And it seems we were
   just acting.
Actors on a stage—that is
   my life
The stage now left empty
Without new music
Without new players
And I continue to cry
For each day that you are
         missing.

In disbelief at the complexities
That surround each one of us
I search the stage for
    someone
But you're not there and
    there are no others.

The show has been closed.
Everyone has gone home
To be alone—
And I remain the only
    player
On the whole stage.

Lost

The path of the leafy forest
  beckons me.
You lead the way and I'm happy.
We find horses outside a small ranch house
And we walk through a circuitous path
That helps me see you as human—
We got lost that day; do you
    remember?

I eat candy with you halfway
  through
From our backpacks and we rest
On the picnic tables we found.
We are somewhere on Long Island.
I was somewhere deeply in love with
  you—
Did you know I loved that day and
  you—
Getting lost together in the woods?

The path we take emotionally is
  different.
You run while I stay far behind.
You run and try to let go of me;
Has our love gotten that heavy?
Has our love become a burden
Without a path that is straight?

And although I never meant
    to lose you
You now know I never believed
    any man
Has truly wanted to keep me;
Yet you I now believe.

And you say I've lost
    my way,
And that you simply don't
    feel the love
And don't trust my love
    any more
Yet I can't give you anything
        more
Than my heart.

I know you may not be mine
    any more.
Your path has veered away
    from mine
And I tried not to see you
    leave.

I stand alone, lost; really lost
In the deepest woods of my
    life
Trying to love myself,
Yet unable to stop loving you too.

Am I lost
Or on your path without a clue?
I feel like I'm chasing you
Through wide open fields
As you dodge me
Telling me to move on
    away from you,
But I never expected
To travel the path alone.

Soul Dance

No more lies, no more sly
    remarks.
Our quirks too much for either
    to bear—
Yet I dream of you and forget,
And go on dreaming while awake;

I tear apart all my reasons
For not being the wife you
    wanted—
And I tear apart my heart
    and the love—
The love I felt and still
    feel.

I am a dreamer, a perfectionist
Seeing things in your eyes that
    you've never known;
Finding parts of you you've never
    shown.
Maybe I'm deluding myself—
Fixing you into the man I dreamed
    you'd be
Or maybe in God's time it's all
    possible.

I do not know; I didn't know
God's time is so slow and difficult.
I burn with desire that's
    unquenchable.
I burn with the sex you gave—
I burn knowing it's in you—the animal.
The sensual man—the beast
That keeps emotions at bay now—

Maybe you don't even know
    or see—
Have you ever thought of me
    that way?
I want to strip you naked to
    the soul.
I want you to let go and let
    me in-
I want to go soul dancing
    with you
Before it's all over—
Before it's too late
To try again.

Smoke

The smoke drifts slowly
   out of his mouth
As his eyes scan the
   distance
Through the steamy night air
Reminding me of the way lovers
Might end the night with
   one last cigarette
In the hope to keep time
   standing still
After that peaceful feeling
   of climax—

I release all thoughts
Into another place and time,
Feeling all your soft caresses
All your delectable touching
Of skin against mine.
Heart beats the only sound.
I want to smoke that smoke.
I want to feel the
   slowness
Of time moving in milliseconds,
Feeling your breath
Against my cheek
Like smoke that settles
Gently bonding,
Endlessly travelling
Mixed with the night
      air.

More Stop Shorts

Children playing
With the sprinkler
Fill the birdbath.

Obsessed
Can't stop thinking
5 AM.

Amidst our conversation
The hummingbird feeds.

The little girl
Feels love
As I feed her.

Wind whipping
The coming storm
The couple kiss.

Medication
Not working yet
As tears fall.

The same word spoken
Then they laugh
Two people.

For Creighton Berry

I claim
Your art
Berry
Almost a name
I knew
In poetry
But no—
Not the same
Berry.

I claim
To love Italy
As much as you.
I know I've never been
But hope
To see
The beauty
You've captured
On canvas.

I have dreams
That you have painted.
I have feelings
You've also captured.

I am in Italy
When I see your "Burano".

I am in Italy
When I see your smile.

"I love it" I say
And you stand proud.

"I'm buying it" I say
And Ivan is floored.

I know your vision
Because I have dreamed
Your canvas, your art.

Age & Love

--for King

The dog hobbles.
His age shows.
He's cute as a puppy
But feels his 11 years.
I kiss and hug him.
I talk to him.
I think he knows
He's loved.

He eats his dinner
And actually
Gets energy
To run & play
In the living room.

This is his
Best part of the day,
And I kiss his head
And his tail wags;
Then he burps
And slows down
   again
To lying down
Under his plant
Or on the carpet
And I kiss him
   again.

I think he knows
That he's loved.
I think he can tell.
I wash him
So he'll look great.
Beige fur brushed.
Teeth cleaned.
He's ready for a show.
For all the neighborhood
To know
Though he hobbles
Through his walks
  now
He is always loved.

Runaway

My life has been a
   runaway run-on sentence
I invite all who participate
   with me
To appreciate its vivaciousness
And to not be too concerned
At my lack of commas
   periods apostrophes and dashes
I am much too busy living
   it to punctuate
Although my mom a former
   educator has her concerns
We laugh at times remembering
That I am not writing
   history books
As that is her favorite topic
I am and will always be
   a poet

Echoes

Echoes of times gone by,
Echoes of Eddie, Roman,
Adam and Jodie,
Laughing, drinking and
Concerts all many years
    ago.
We were close, we were
    bonded
By our trust of each
    other.
Time has flown
And we have disbanded,
Some married, some
    moved away,
But a smile is on
    my face
As I remember the love
We all shared for each other.

47772688R00055